The Wild Rantings
of a Teenage Girl

AESHA WAKS

Order this book online at www.trafford.com
or email orders@trafford.com

Most Trafford titles are also available at major online book retailers.

Print information available on the last page.

ISBN: 978-1-4907-7596-8 (sc)
ISBN: 978-1-4907-7595-1 (e)

Trafford rev.   08/23/2016

 www.trafford.com
North America & international
toll-free: 1 888 232 4444 (USA & Canada)
fax: 812 355 4082

During the time this book was written, I had my lovely mom, Mindy Waks, Grandmother, Sylvia Metzger and grandfather, Wolfgang Metzger around. I would like to thank them in heaven for all of their love, inspiration and support. They taught me the point of living is to never give up on my dreams and do my best to use the skills that I have to make this world a better place.

I would also like to thank my family, especially Israel, Geffen and Gigi Waks for always being there to make me smile, and my friends, especially Thea Samuelson, Andre Joseph, Tennie Leonard, Donna Murphy, John Buffalo Mailer, Debbie and Marilyn Gelfand, Bradley Kaplan, Devin Ratray and Donna Murphy to name a few that have been there for me always, but most importantly recently. Thank you for always believing in me.

Amidst our rehearsals on set for the film Smoke Screen, in which I play the role of contract killer Emma Pierce, I noticed this book, used as a prop, the Goetia. I asked director Sean Buttimer about it and he told me that it was a dark magic book written by Aleister Crowley. Oddly enough, this inspired me to dig through my collections and put out my own book as an actress. Crowley was known as a very powerful yet evil man, but holding his book in my hands somehow provoked me to want one of my own, to express who I am. Sometimes the strangest things, good or evil, can inspire something positive to happen and I tend to try to find the good in everything I can. Take this as you wish. Sean, thank you for being one of the most important people I could have met and also taking the time to give a final edit.

Jared Leto

I made my dad split an ecstasy tab with me
At a club
Called the Mirage
While Jared Leto asked me to write my phone
number
On a cocktail napkin
By the bar
My mom was the designated driver
Jared called
The next day
As I sat on the steps leading to my basement
Red carpet leading
Downstairs...

Wedding vows

Through sleep
Through wealth
Through boredom do us part
I plan to die on the moon
Come with me
Be it too soon.

Long To Play

She stepped off the bus
A recorder in hand and she knew
But didn't know how
And didn't know when she'd get through
She was reading Lolita
Like candy you'll eat her
She's who

Long to play
Everyday
In every way
She'll come through

Like a marionette
Wig on her head
Powder blue
She dances her dance
While she throws off romance
If you knew
Don't care about gossip
No skeleton closet
She's through

Long to play
Everyday
In every way
She'll come through

Creating a space
Then they come to her place
Two by two
Healing your soul
And will never get old
Though some do
Turn the world right side up
Like the way our father wanted to

Long to play
Everyday
In every way
She'll come through

Blue

His eyes of blue, he don't know what to do about me
If he only knew, the one thing, I don't want to be
free
His long lashes bat
He looks down to the ground
Don't know what to say
But he'll see me one day
And he prays
But in the meanwhile
Thieves of my virginity
Benefactors of my virility lurk and work to take me
away from him
They claw, and they beg
They break their own legs over me
Sometimes I don't know if it's worth it to sin
Give me one reason for you and I to begin
Oh rescue me
Tell me you're the only one for me

His smile is innocent
If he only knew I thought it was mint
If he only knew to take my hint
He kisses me with fear in his lips
The fear of losing would never be missed
For no one would be ever dissed
But in the meanwhile
While I stay so cool and undemanding
Un-possessive and understanding
I freeze in the cold arms of another
While distant thoughts of him hover
And fade 'til the calendar says it's okay
And I see him with a warm new day
Just take me away
Rescue me from this parade
Tell me that everything's okay

His legs are solid
If it would only dare to take a stand
Tell me what he wants
'cause every day I'm more in demand
His hands are strong
But I'm mercury
So hold on to me
I'm flesh and bones and heart and I'm being ripped
apart
But in the meanwhile
For now or later
Live your life now
And you'll benefit later
I said I love who loves me the most
Don't let the rest fool me to get close
Fame
Money
Passion
The poetry
I love who loves me most
Don't ever let me go, in summer or in snow

Nexus

I'm in the Nexus
Pumping you like oil in Texas
Glad you met this?
Trying hard to get this?
Wet this?
I'll bet this
Imma wreck this
I'm reckless
Writing checks, bitch
While they playing Tetris
I'm straight edge and shit
While your coke whore got arrested
Just for another meth fix
While priests are blessing this
She's praying for her next lift

Top floor
Open doors
Make love not war
All fours
Never bored
Strike like a cord
Tongue like a sword
He think I'm a whore
But it's me they adore
Put zombies in an uproar
Bad to the core
Keep going, just when you thought I got no more

Grey

Sometimes it's well and good to be
Shady
It's never too yes or too no
It's just maybe

Never too happy
Never too sassy
Never too sad
Enough to be classy
But
Grey is safe
It's encompassing
Enough not to be a disgrace
Grey is just warm
Enough to be cold
Cool enough
Not to be jealous
If it's mixed right
Never puts up a fight
Avoids too dark
Or too light
It's surface calm
But deep inside
Grey
Is
Black and white

Black

Out of the shadows
I fly
Like the crow
Endless energy at night
I know
High beams from my eyes
Show
People let loose
To songs of gin sloe
There is a curtain of energy
In the air
When it's black
Gods eye is shut
And I never look back
Flying high above the streets
I conquer
I move
I soar
I screech

The object

Like a tree encased in leaves
Or a bird endowed with feathers
I stand alone these city streets
With jet black hair in tethers

With silver pointed corsets
Metallic platform shoes
Ruffled mini skirts, striped sequent tights
And lustrous scarves of blue

I walk along these city streets
All eyes bug out at me
That wild finesse
That I pose
Explodes and I'm set free

Cupids knock

Tick
Tick
Tick
Tock
Hear the beating rhythm lock
Time is flying
Make it stop
Guard the pulsing
Thumping
Clock

Golden cupid
Standing locked
Stop the drumming
Make it stop
Time is melting
Wrinkles drop
Wings are sprouting
Halos pop

Let the aging process stop
Time is measured
On the clock
Space less time
Exploding rock
Time goes on till cupid knocks

Billy Idol

Hidden bar
Secret lounge
Leather couches
Sculpted round

Called over
By the sweetest man in town
Following day
Limo pulled onto my grounds

Seated in my own section
To hear my ears greatest perfection
I was serenaded to White Wedding
In such a private and grand setting

"You're the girl Billy sang to"
I'm Aesha but who are you?
Pete Townshend he said
I'm the Who...
Whoops....

Rebel

I feel like
Everything is backwards
Catholic schoolgirls
Bunch up and tear thru
Their
Uniform
To show
Individuality
Like clothes
Like minds
And then...
A rebel emerges
Out of
The seeds
Of
Similarity

I was born
On a mushroom
I was born
A fully emerged rebel
I spend my days
Looking for
Similarities
Between us
But
My brain and vessel
Cannot
Fit
In
The
Box
I am stuffing myself in
How
Obvious
I look

When will north and south
Winds
Connect
To find a happy medium of
Normalcy exploring
And
Exploring normalcy
"You're crazy"
Beside
Reading all statements
Backwards
To try to find hidden
Meanings
And the fact
That I speak
Gibberish
When I'm upset
Oh yeah
I also consider religion
To be metaphysics
Other than that

If you can pinpoint your differences
That's all it is
It's being consciously different
If I put on a uniform
And keep my mouth shut
I'll probably look
Like I'm about to explode
"You're crazy"
Do I look bad
Even writing about this?
Or should we analyze all of the available answers for
the statement "You're crazy"
"That's crazy"
That's a very small word coming from an even
smaller person

Weed

When I daze off into the corner
With blank and unfilled intentions
Your aura sometimes comes to me
And it visits
And it takes me on a trip

I can't see the walls and the ceiling
I can't hear the people speaking to me
I can't smell the smoke filled room
And I forget about my other two senses

We are here now
Floating mid air
With the thought of your spirit guiding me
Through my meditation
It feels peaceful
Yet violently outraged
Light as I float through the clouds
But dark as I walk through the forest
And found you lying in the leaves with arms
extended
I see myself helping you up
And walk to an empty dirt road
In the desert
With cactus
And your bag flung over your shoulder
Your hitching thumb tucked
Deep in your pocket

Walking beside yourself
With your head forward
And you're precise about going you don't know
where but you're sure wherever it is it will be
Right
Now

Prologue

To:
All worlds that come down here
And show us another view
I thank you
For showing me another side
To my image that moves through the mirror
Dancing and smiling
Like Alice In Wonderland
Can you reach out and touch me one day?
To the reflections in the glass
Seeing like there is something transparent
And what we can see and not touch
Oh outer world you are right there
All we have to do is open our imaginations

Comradery

Who is ready for love?
Cupid will one day hunt us down
And shoot us and that arrow will point to us
With that rare untimely magic it possesses
And then you will be marked for the hunting
Some of us pray for his shot
Some of us run
But don't you try to ever think you can shoot
yourself
And take away his job
And this is why I will entitle this poem
Comradery

Triple A

My rhymes blow up your ride
Gotta call Triple A
My rhymes blow up your lies
Gotta watch what you say
My lines are like blow
You get addicted to my taste
My daily affirmations
Don't let them go to waste
Cause if you catch on, messages will come from
grace

Gotta give to get that's infinite
Or you'll come back as a twisted infant
Have you screamin' out the womb like a serpent
reincarnate
You know me like fire
Like it when I'm rough
Sensitive artists get whipped
Till their skin turns tough
I'll have you beggin' and pleadin' for my innocent
poems
Industry screamin' for original resolutions for their
lows
I'll fog up your windows with contradicting cons and
pros
Unintentional hurt comes from truth
Not low blows
Get your bullet proof vest
Cause my mouth shoot down NO'S

Crumbalin down

I wanna stay so cool while your crumbalin down
Cause you know you're testin' me when you picking
up sound
You know you drivin' me crazy
So I pump on your break
Because you makin' me frantic
So I start makin' mistakes

I'll be hard as a rock
As you cracking alone
I wont ever let you move me
I'll be still as stone
I wont let you shake me down, boy
Cause that would be a sin
But the last time you pissed me off
That wont happen again

Come together

All of us come together
As one
All God's children
Daughters and sons

You ma'am, therefore are my sister and you sir, my
brother
Jesus is also my brother
And Mary my mother

I'm not looking for love
I'm looking and searching for all of my brothers
reunite and the solar system of souls I once knew
when

But lets not get too deep
So take back your flowers and flattery that showers
I don't want it
I'm not shot
I'm roaming

Spain

The sun was setting in a small town in Spain, and caused a halo effect on the Adobe rooftops. There was a dishwasher spraying down the sparkling cobblestone streets, to get them ready for the dinner crowd...till the ground looked like gray clay. This was a very private restaurant, found in a discrete alleyway, and in the dark all you could hear are the whispers of sinners and clinks of wine glasses. During the day, people would salsa in the streets, there under the sun, laugh, get high on caffeine, and plan their rendezvous for the evening. At night, they would come there to dine and proceed to the exclusive hotel atop of the cellar nightclub. The only way to get in was to entertain the doorman, with a private, exciting reservation, and mention the names of people that they would not like in there that evening. After showing their ID, and slipping him a one hundred dollar bill.

But for now, it was still sunset, innocent, still sprayed-down, sparkling clay roads by the dishwasher. There was a click-clack, click-clack coming toward him. He was too shy to look up, so he closed his eyes, and as the wind blew through his hair, sweat dripped down his brow. He began fantasizing about the woman about to appear. He then courageously opened his eyes, to witness his true fantasy. Slowly and bravely raised his head, but realized he has sprayed the senorita with his hose. Dripping on her white stiletto heels first, then to her long white wedding gown-like dress, then to her now brown wavy hair and red glossy lipstick, she was his perfection. She then picked up the hose, sprayed him right back, giggled, and clicked away to find whatever sunlight was left for her to dry. She went to find the club that you would only know about if you were a dishwasher or having an affair.

People were all over each other, doing the lambada, wives of husbands of mistresses of scandal, the dishwasher followed her in. By the time she got there, William left her standing by herself. The dishwasher was watching her. She left the club and entered the alleyway. The dishwasher though to himself, "she came for me, she left for me." He followed after her. She starts giggling and running. "This is a fun game," he thought. So excited, so happy to be alive, he yells out, "I love you, seniorita!" She picked up her long, white train, and starts running faster, but this time she yells out, "I love you!"

The dishwasher runs faster and pins her up against the wall, where she stopped. He finally has her, his heart is beating, he is about to get his real first kiss. When he suddenly hears, "I love you, too, Lena," as a rose falls from a balcony up above. And there is William, waiting, adorned with sunglasses, robe, and two glasses of red. He thanks the dishwasher for bring Lena to him safely, and throws him a one-hundred dollar bill. "Dishwasher, and that's for not telling anybody you saw us together." Her love was not for the dishwasher, her love was not for William, her love was not for anyone. La vida loca, her love for life.

The streets of cobblestone, they sparkle and shine, the sunshine reflects on rooftops, it looks like golden lines. And there he is at the end of the road, arms exposed to the light of her soul, waiting down on one knee, for a night of ecstasy. The people of the town, they danced until nightfall came down. The outdoor café gets them so high, they want to cry. There he was, ready for whatever. And she was so scared that it might last forever. Then he left, and gave her what she wanted, but little did she know that she couldn't really live without him. The marble water fountain cries that she is without him. She puffs upon a cigarette, hopes the smoke will make her choke. Why was she so pressured by this man? And now he left on her last chance. She didn't know it was the last. He is lost. She'll never see his face again. She feels like every other lover. The streets of cobblestone, they will continue to sparkle every day. The Adobe houses, they will still be made of clay. This town will always make her cry, she will never say goodbye.

Shake

Come here now, have a taste
Commit, I'd rather date
Come drink ya ice cream shake
Same thing my daddy make

Hold up while ya make that face
So what, I take a break from grace
Shake that, let me break that waist
Play back, let me have that taste

I'm rockin' dark Crip blue, Blood red, and
chartreuse too
Nikes, my top J Crew
Hair messed up with molding glue

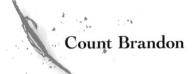

Count Brandon

Where
Was I that night?
Some afterhours
Filled with Eurotrash slaves
Looked like some graffitied up bat cave
We better behave...

Went there with Dracula (or so I said)
His teeth were like fangs
He used as a pen (or so he said)
His words like red ink
And like red blood he bleeds words
On my flesh paper he fed (as he said)

I was intrigued by his face and that place
The 2 at once made my cold heart race
His eyes as blue as the sky
During an eclipse
The black against white
Shadowed the light

He scorched himself
With the burning flames of my cigarette
Like the fire that I am
Aesha means fire back in the holy land

Oh look over there
It's a crackhead!
Oh is that a crack den?
And what's that, a bathtub?
Yes, that's what we saw
Ok better get out of here
But first wouldn't you like another cup of 16 dollar
bourbon?
So the English barmaid could buy her one way ticket
out of here?
No
Didn't think so

Cest la vie

Just picture this
We driving down the highway
In the wild, wild west
With wind in our hair
And we don't give a fuck
No we don't really care
Cause you stressin' us out and we up and out of here
Cause we going to there
A vacation to nowhere
To forget our name
Street fame, have no fear

Cause when you get no rest or self-introspection
It's like life fucked you with out protection
Like a big 'ol ground hog day injection
Better get out before you get an infection
Better get out before the lord shakes you with a
breakdown
Spins you with a black out or maybe a shakedown
Feelin' like you loosin' your mind
Like trepidation
Better dip into the next train
Right out of the station
Last car to nowhere
You feel like your trail blazin'
Cause my mind's hallucinations are having me
shakin'

True Love

True love is hard to find
Do you want me or are you just out to get me?
You know you have two sides
One is for me and the other is blind
Don't try to waste my time
If you're not all there, I don't want you to be mine
Don't have to be ashamed, that the bad part of you,
likes me when I'm not tamed

When you see, that we
Aren't gonna stay this way
Cause the devil in you
Wants the devil in me
It doesn't have to go away

I want your bad side
To want my bad side
She'll never hurt you
Unless I want to
Unless you don't ride
And no you can't hide
I never could lie
But I want your bad side
To love my bad side

Clock

The clock keeps tickin'
My mind keeps leakin'
Body keeps freakin'
I need that inspiration
Your rhymes
Your rhymes
They keep me going

In this time of darkness
Could there be stillness
Sincere divine
Could there be love amongst
Competitive fields
The rat race filled with lies
Could we climb to the top of the mountain?
And still survive
Or will we spontaneously combust
Simultaneously as we hide

Girls love

It seems like every single girl
Love a thug with a glock
Doo rag you can see him all the way down the block
With his hand on his jock
Wrist iced up with rocks
Tattoos, throwbacks, pants down to his socks

Seem like every player get with the confidence proves
clear evidence of self-acceptance
When you love yourself
Everyone will next
Take a chance, a romance, and respect yourself

They talkin' bout slow motion
When you know New York's fast forward
I half time it in the booth
Cause my hearts pumpin' and flowin'
Cause I'm livin' it up like I'm in the wild west
Downin' JB you know it warm up my chest
Lasso on my waist
Bullet proof is my vest
Reality is my test
Bring it on who's next

Stephano from 725 park ave.

Went to a party
Invite by new friend
Came in solo
Then I met him
Left captured...and surprised

His presence was intimidating
He was dashing
He had an army of souls behind him

His eyes black
No
Blue
If you had the courage to look into them
Slight build
Short messy hair
He danced without a care
He treated me sweetly
To everything
I wanted nothing
He hugged
And kissed me
He felt like no stranger
He called me little Bebe
Don't call people names
He called
We'll see him again

CAT

Dark as midnight
At times you cause me fright
In dead sleep
At times I feel your bite
In my dreams
A stranger in the light

Are the myths really true?
Can you cross a path and have salt be threw?
Are you evil in your innocent ways?
Like bad luck and jinxes do?
Do your teeth draw blood?
Do your eyes pierce through and through?

Or are you an angel in black mink?
Do you make the mind just reel and think?
Painted darker than white or pink
Can you be the missing link?

Or is it that we can't grow attached to you
Reminding us of the cat that we once knew
Who we poured our love onto
Got swept away into the blue

Or are you the one that grounds our home
Will you be with us until we are grown?
Can you bring us joy with your litter and turkey
bones?
Can you enter our days so that we are never alone?

Dirty

Drunken
Dirty fingernails
Smokey
Sick
Sad
Rancidly thin
Self-motivated
Growing out hair
Sour feeling
Dry puffy eyes
Like a baby crab being washed ashore
I long for the tides
To wash me back in
To home
I had enough learning on shore
For now
Maybe some left?!
Perch me on a rock in the frontal ocean
For now
Until I learn to swim
And let me cry part of the ocean
That surrounds me and bless it with comfortable
element of self
Till I become one with the water
And let my soul fly about me
Cause I'm safe now in my ocean of tears
The water will be safe soon to go back in
Pretty soon
I'll learn how to swim

SEX

Sex to me is rare and bare
Our secrets told, I'll never share
Don't fuck me once
But love me twice
Don't make it bland
Throw on some spice
Don't be so wild
But drive me wild
Choose a role
Adult
Or child
For innocence is bliss
Experience strong as a fist

My poetry and music
Keeps me from going insane
I'll smoke a cigarette like a chain
My pain is vain
But not to disdain
Don't leave me hangin' like a chain
You like it dirty
I'll give you clean
You like control
I'll be the dean
You act too nice
And
I'll be mean

Oh poor confusion
I beset
You be my master
I'll be your pet
For balance is the key to life
You lick me once
I'll bite you thrice

CONTROL

Then one day
You noticed him
Now he's all shady
Like you can't win
Your Id is blinded from light to dim
You now like him
You feel you've sinned

Then element of self-surprise
U lost control
Then realize
That you are the followed
You are the prize
You are the one that caught his eyes

Write

I write of what oppresses my soul
I spend my days fulfilling the prophecies
Of my dues
I collect the moments
Of freedom to write

I pay my dues to become one of an actress
Or one of a key master
A key to open a door
A door called freedom

Some go for this door directly
Some marry the door
I shalt not
God hath given me many gifts
I will mold my iron
I have become a proverbial
Blacksmith and will make my key

The door is finally creaking
I will stick with it
And have become one of an object-thing
Soon I will be ready to
Fully unlock the door
I will then step through
And secretly become one of a writer

One of a simple dancer
Is not enough to fulfill my dreams
One of an actress is not enough
To fulfill what God hath given me
One of a director is not enough to fulfill my soul
Yet one of a writer is enough to act as a median
And have angels speak through me

I will take mental mathematics and apply that to my
heart-mind-soul
And become in time a voice to teach every how to
listen to theirs

Positive

If my so-called life can be started after 21
My prediction is right
No more every night parties
Smoking
Messing around with many men
Indulging
Trying everything for myself

Then why shouldn't I enjoy the chaos now?
I have much to look forward to
Waking up the same time every day
With a schedule

Look at all you have to look forward to
Filling up moments with what I think would be
pleasurable

SPARKLE

The diamonds in the streets of NYC
Sparkled like broken glass
An old man turns his head
To find out if I'm stalking
So he waits till I pass

I took my 2:00 breakfast
As I ride backwards on the train
I think of what will now go in my favor
Or drive me insane

Nick from O'Neills

O'Neills 10 pm enter bar:
Co-workers and pseudo-friendly gentleman asks me
for a cigarette (on these occasions I am glad that I
smoke)
He was tall
In shape
Cheekbone length
Black hair
To match his black getup
And silver hoop earing
Well-defined features
He spoke shyly
"Can I bum a smoke?" what's your name (I said)?
He says are you here with pseudo?
Sit with me, I know your friend (he says)
We will probably speak more because we don't have
each other's numbers (I thought)
Later (says I)

But low and behold, he joined us anyway
With his smokey brown eyes he gazed at me smiling
I work for Aerosmith (he says)
Are you coming to dinner (I said)
Yes (he said)
And so the 10 of us sat down and swallowed some
wounded elephants
The last thing we said to each other was yes I'm
shy in general-me too, I hopped on the back of my
friend's bike and treaded downtown
Never saw him again
We lost each other
In the streets of NYC

FLOATING

Like you're floating in space
Darkness
Eyes closed
Sitting
But falling down
Standing
But falling back
You're not here
But you are
Personal thoughts make you laugh
Cry until you get it out of you
And become numb
Exactly in life
Like a mannequin
You have the control to speak
Or move
Or be still
Let the vibrations reflect off your body
And your energy exit through your limbs
Your soul is now your puppet
Mind/body control
Is with your higher power in trust and faith

SWEET MUSIC

She lulls him to sleep with her sweet music
Takes him places beyond his world/lyrics and physics
Lost in his imagination
He is king of his domain
But he has saved no money for when it rains
She has built him castles made of pillows
Where he can manifest his dreams
He dreams in sun lit yellow
But when he wakes his world is black
But she tells him black is nothing and nothing is where it's at
She has painted a world and it's the only world to live
And she says happiness is never given it's taken
And what you take you have to give
Come step into hope she tells him
Your visions will appear, come live in hopes dimension
For your future's already here

The Midnight Hour
(From the Angelina Jolie produced film "Lovesick")

The Clock struck 12
No one could make me go to bed
And I had an idea that my memories would soon be fed
Band-Aids are temporarily my life
Tobacco and sugar
Now my med
To only live in the present
Don't let the now be dead
Let answers and keys be known
Again and again I said
Release the knowledge now
Immediately
So I can go to bed

My room adorned in club style
Swinger
Candles
Music fled
Sweet oh man in my bed
Mannequin style
Fleetwood mac
Silent stead

Wake up wake up
Play the role of my club
Listen to my poem be read
Play with me till dawn
Don't let your head be like lead
Let my mind be your zed

July don't
Won't
Hear my song
So it fills my heart
With empty long
Oh be with me in my moment of need
Hear my cry you sleepy steed

When I am up
You are down
When I am down
You are a clown
When will I ever savor the pleasure of endless
moments and words that clever
So savor the moments now or leave us
Fill your lungs with smoke achieve us
Pleasure the splendor of time it is sublime for the
very few we are together
But I haven't a clue

Where are those poetic moments on the beach I preach?
Your creativity unleash
My mind is like bleach
I'm painting with glue of what's ahead
Please oh please don't make me go to bed
I want to be at peace with Zed
Oh pain oh pain
I emp. The dead
I wake up startled in my bed
I cry for fulfillment in my little head
Off in your dream world
Tomorrow you cry
Cigarettes are like drugs for my mind
Ill let them go in time
What a crime
When summer is over ill turn a leaf of fall
Soul at peace but bodies cry
Oh, serpent of the day
Leave your prey to fray at night
Hold onto me like a kite
I bite the night with no fright
I suck it through my candlelight
Like a vampire
Its blood will bring you life

Be good boys and girls
When fall ignites
Its still summer
Abuse its delight
Find your soul alone at night
Search for the light
I'm sure with me
You'll delight

Oh sleep oh sleep
I like this world
When I know it will leave out of site
Hold me now
Connect your body and soul without fright
Please conquer me night
Stop no don't!

POST TEEN…

God

If there's a god up there
Then he's wearing a chain
He's black, white, yellow, red, he's rockin' a cane.
His glittering moon
His starry hall of fame
Look up at the sky, I think he's tagging his name.
He could be vane, He created Gucci
That's why we rhyme about money, fame, power,
coochie.
He speak through many
Puffy, Jay and Kanye
And on a blessed night, he might come and
touch me.
That's why they thank him when they win an award
'Cause God's writing rap songs when he gets bored

Oh God, why are you ticklin, teasin'
Since a minute ago you got my mind easin'
Feel your energy flowing throughout my pen
Don't know what I'm writing, I'm just following
my pen
Oh shit, don't even mind if I curse
These fucking words is part of your universe
Oh shit, God, am I going too far?
Is the Devil taking over and fighting on my
shoulder?

Wanna take me to a bar and light me a cigar?
Stop, fight, I think I'm going to war
Stop, breathe, I think I'm thinking too hard
I'm not even coking, ecstasy-ing or blazing
When I focus on you, my mind just starts racing
Let go like a free fall
Heart like a b-ball
Praying to you is like making a collect call
Wait, stop, my stomach's aching
Or is it just a sign that you're done with your painting?
God's everything, a virgin and perverted
Why else mini-skirts, to keep the heads turning?
All the ass in the video keep the men burning
Temptation, God, it keeps the men yearning.
God's got humor, he laughs his guts out
And breaks out the Chrystal
VIP's his crowd
And you know he got style in his throwback robes
'cause when he lifts up his jammies, he's got Nike's on his toes.
A different angel every day of the week
Drinking a lot of Starbuck's 'cause he never sleeps
God must love rap, 'cause it ain't the Devil
Deep within our father lies a cause and a rebel

-M0M-

Where was I?
When angels came to steal you?
Lifted you above the ground so high
I know one day that I will come to see you
Even though it won't be till I die

The moments in between your breath
Not
Frequent
Every
One
You
Take
May
Be
Your
Last

Since your coma fell
You have not spoken
Angels of the Lord
Please
Take
Her
Fast

Don't want you to go
But you're not here
Don't remember the last time that you smiled
Walked
Ate
Drank
Danced
Talked
Sang
It turned you back into a child

Breathed in...
But she didn't breath out
No one saw a difference
Two months
She lay out
No
Words
No food
In her mouth
Two months
Two months
Went by in a bed in our house
Withering away
Doubts

Fear
Pain
Love
Rain
Family crowds around
Grandma screams her name
Soul
Lifted up to the heavens
Body lifted
Why did I miss it?

Grabbed her hand
Her arm
Her wrist
It went limp
Grabbed her face
And I kissed it
Put my head on her chest
It was empty
Skin cold
I knew she was home

Mystery

He walked into my life as from out of nowhere
Where did I find u I really don't care
Where did u go to
I want to know u

Love at first site
Could not be real
Where did they hide u
We stayed away, but looked real close and
I tried to deny you
You are my mystery man
Following mystery plans
Oh my mystery man
Dreaming, forming mystery lands

Be my mystery girl
I'll wrap you up in diamonds and pearls
Oh my mystery girl
Bringing me to new mystery worlds

U try to defy the spirits that fly
But angels still guide u
Gave me your light
Put up a fight
Now I'll never deny u

This mystery miss
Seems to me to be elusory
This lady of shroud
Needs to find ways 2 blend into the crowd

Mystery girl(man)where have u been, all of my life,
all of my life has been, been being wasted when I
caught his eye he gave me a try
And I knew he adored me

Gave me a stage, lifted my cage and he did it all
for me
The world tried to hide me, tried to deny me, not
ready for me
He lifted me high, shot out his light, now they
cannot ignore me

Fewer For Me

If you give me a taste of your bottle
Maybe we'll know if I know you tomorrow
We'll see
Fewer for me

If you call me day in and day out
And then I call you, will you run out?
We'll see
Fewer for me

If I start talking dirty to you
Then will you freak out, not know what to do?
We'll see
Fewer for me

If I tell you that you are my friend
Will you go out, hook up with my friends?
We'll see
If you are for me

If I show my hand
Will you comprehend?
Show you where it hurts
Will you know my worth?

I put myself out there over and over again
(over and over and over and over again)

You're stepping to me
I'm stepping to you
Step up you're game, cause I'm getting ahead
You're doing all the right things, thinking that will
send me to bed
Keeping things so cool, I think I'm cooling off
So cold, so bled, don't try to turn me off
I'll light a fire, fuck myself, at least I'm not dead

Infinity, infinity, infinity, in front of me again
I'm outing myself, outta respect
Respect to get read

If I show my hand
Will you comprehend?
Show you where it hurts
Will you know my worth?

Submission

With my hands on your dishes
Keep me in your kitchen
I pay for admission
With my sweet submission

When I talk you don't listen
My job is your bitchin'
My soul you'll be missin'
I'm leaving, I'm itchin'

It's my time to do the ditchin'
I'm throwing in my mittens
Your life's already been written
This seems to be real fittin'

Your words make me feel bitten
I'm tired of all your hittin'
I know you used to be smitten
But now you're only reaching for the gun

I gotta get away
You say some things that really put me down
And when I leave, won't even make a sound

Money can't buy you submission
You want me bare in the kitchen
No you won't listen to bitchin'
You think you so rich and

Money can't buy you submission
When I talk, you don't even listen
Always looking so pissed and
But when I leave I'll be missed

Now I got one little thing to say right now
Money won't make me bow

Money can't buy you submission
You think you raising a fist and
Will make me actually listen
When you should be doing more kissin'

Money can't buy you submission
When I'll be doing the dissin'
Yes it is me you'll be missin'
And that's a lot you'll be riskin'

Money don't buy you love but it'll buy me things
when you screw me over
Money don't buy you love but it'll buy me things
when the love is over

Drip It Like Waks

I drip
I drip it like Waks
I drip it like Waks

Late night
When nobody can see me
And you're in your bed dreamin'
That's when I come creepin' up through your fire
escape

Right through your window
And I see you through your pillow
And I grab one of your candles
Right off of your mantel

I walk over to your bed
And I stand over your head
Hold that candle up high
Just hope you don't cry!

I drip
I drip it like Waks
I drip it like Waks

Late night
I like to suck your neck
On your terrace in the rain
Cause you know it gets me wet as it's drippin' down
callin' out my name

Like Waks
I'm giving you the facts
While I'm watching you relax
Takin' you under attack

Don't get stage fright
When I bite
Late night it's alright
When I'm spittin' on the trax
While I'm spinning like Wax

I drip
I drip it like Waks
I drip it like Waks

Tomorrow

How can we make it through tomorrow?
Can we, can we, can we fill this hole?
Can we, can we, can we rid our sorrows?
Without, without getting down too low

How do we not go beg or borrow?
Can we, can we, can we live alone?
Can we, can we, can we rid our sorrows?
Without, without getting down too low

Without getting down too low
Without getting down too low
Without getting down
You know I like to get down
And when I'm down I like to take it slow

I'll ride my car out there tomorrow
I don't care if I beg or borrow
I'm tryna rid myself of sorrow
Without getting down too low

I'll never half way through my way through
I like to do one thing at a time
I'll figure out the key
And who is meant for me
Without without getting down too low

Can you please, can you please, can you please
Help my sister
Can you please, can you please, can you please
Help my friend
Can you please, can you please, can you please
Help my sister
Can you please, can you please, can you please
Help my sister free

I'm in a prison in my own mind
Help me help me help me break on free
Setting up my own mistakes
Livin' up to do what it takes
Without without getting down too low

You know that justice just moved in here
And I know your gonna get your karma too
I know you have been feelin' blue but I feel the same
as you
Were gonna get there without feelin' low

Without getting down too low
Without getting down too low
Without getting down
You know I like to get down
And when I'm down I like to take it slow

Andy Hurley

He's not only vegan
But straight edge
Hmm...
I'd like to be straight edge
I'm sick of experimenting with drugs and thugs...

Covered in tattoos and diamonds
I want to be more like you everyday
But you've gone away again
On your tour bus
Do I forget you for now?
Or do I hold on
Will the meaning I put to you
Change and strengthen who we are
Or is the distance what keeps us together...

007 Miri Ben-Ari

Name's Aesha, I'm insatiable
Crime turns me on, Miri plays to kill
She's got the world on a string
Like Sinatra backing Kennedy
Game's a puppet on a string, like the Godfather's
enemy

Hold the violin like it's your 00 gun
And if anyone asks, I know 00 nothing
She's got a license to ill
The deal is 00 done
I'm digging the explosive of your Doublemint Gum

Damn, Miri, you make 'em say what's that?
Make a player hater tip a hat and wanna step back
With your gold finger, everything you touch sings
They say diamonds are forever, but you outlast their
bling

Black snake

When the Black Snake bites
You're gonna feel a fang or two
The black snake's venom
It will really wreck your mind
Take you places where you have never been
Then leave the world behind

It's long
It's dark
And it stays low to the ground
It slithers in silence and it's coming to your town

It's long
It's dark
And it's coming for you
There's only one thing you can do
When the black snake is coming for you

Run
There's a black snake coming
Coming after you
Gonna wrap some black scaly coils
Around you
When you see the black snake
Coming
There is only one thing you can do
You better run, run, run
From the black snake
Run, hide, run from the black snake
Run, hide, run, run, run
Away
Save your life and live another day
Make no mistake
Better run away
From the black snake

Invisible veins

Seduce if she may
A virgin in may
May not you listen
She will make you obey
She will send in her guides
One at a time
Make sure her patient
Crosses that line that leaves behind
Roadblocks, darkness and pain
You'll love her and hate her
Invisible veins

Spirit superior

Spirit superior
Encompassing all
Mixed in with personal
Credited halls
Summoning light
To benefit all

She morphs into shapes that some recognize
And then when it's suited
She wears a disguise
And if it's for granted
She'll seem like a bitch
That gradually fades
When missions not ditched

Existing not time but quick like a motor
Her motives are pure but sure to promote her

Bettie Page Bang

Bang bang
Pick me up with my Bettie Page bangs
So we can hang
Bang bang
Pick me up with my Bettie Page bangs
So we can

Up on stage
Lights on
Camera, action
Nights on
Burlesque
Centerfold
Heart made of
Pure gold
Whips out
Feather boa
Constrictor
Contradictor
Red lipstick
Round hips
Straddle chairs good enough to throw tips at
Leather corset
Black tights
Disco balls
And flashing lights
I picked up cause you rang
Now pick me up with my Bettie Page bangs

Bang bang
Pick me up with my Bettie Page bangs
So we can hang
Bang bang
Pick me up with my Bettie Page bangs
So we can

You and me
From a distance
Up close
Persistence
Like whips and like cuffs
I'm so sweet but you like it when I'm rough
Leather panties
Black nails
Mouth like a garbage pail
Wet like a water bottle
Walk like a super model
Pole dancing
For fun
Strip teasing
For none
I picked up cause you rang
Now pick me up with my Bettie Page bangs

Bang bang
Pick me up with my Bettie Page bangs
So we can hang
Bang bang
Pick me up with my Bettie Page bangs
So we can

Brett Ratner

"Come meet up and hang out with John Cusack"
"Ok"
His piercing blue eyes
Spoke to me over a frosted margarita
As my friend in a booth was tucked away in a deep
conversation
With John
The night drifted by quick as we danced
Smiles worth a thousand words

Deep breath

I don't remember the last time I took a deep breath
Stopped and smelled the roses, I've been so damn
upset
I've yet to feel what could be called peace of mind
Cause every time I unwind guilt gets me grinding

Self-motivated, need no one to tell me to grind
harder
Feet on the pavement so much that they are turning
into mortar
That's great you like my shit but don't criticize me
less you got your construction kit, don't tell me who
to be

My confidence alarming
Maybe I look like a dreamer
I know reality well
You're just an extra in my feature
Not just a girl, more of a creature
Outer planetary soul
And sometimes a preacher

Don't need a crew of wimps to tell me to do the
right thing
So many doubts, so negative they are frightening
I like to rage, I'm scandalous, I've done bugged out
I've penetrated page 6 before Paris' video come out
I displayed to Maxim magazine what oral sex to pizza
is all about
Cover of the Daily News fist fighting dudes in a
crowd
Well maybe that was a movie, but so is my life, can't
hold a real job down and I'm no one's wife
Head so far in the clouds that God's like
How's life?
I rest well but when I work it's tight
Might have a temper but I call it spice, and if you
don't like it I'll piss on your face then wipe

No I have no shame and no one to blame
All positive, you wanna call me vain?
I have a whole crew of people that would laugh at
your caution
You can't handle all this
You gotta take me in portions

Vin Diesel

I looked up and saw a man made of stone
Ambition dripping from his biceps and bones
One moment bouncing the door at my favorite club
Making sure I was never alone
Next moment his film at Sundance same year as
mine
Next moment Spielberg on his phone
And like a bolt of lightning he shot up to the sky
One moment holding his hand
Next moment watching him fly

Butterfly

If you touch one butterfly
The world would surely change for the good
But if I just stay a while
And enjoy it while I could